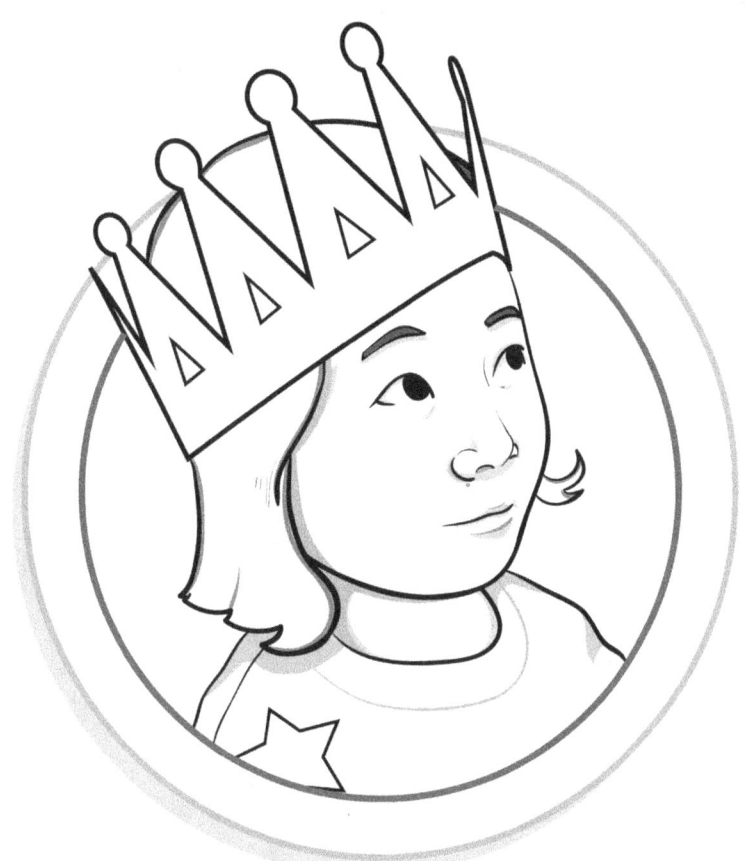

PEMA PLAY COLORING BOOK

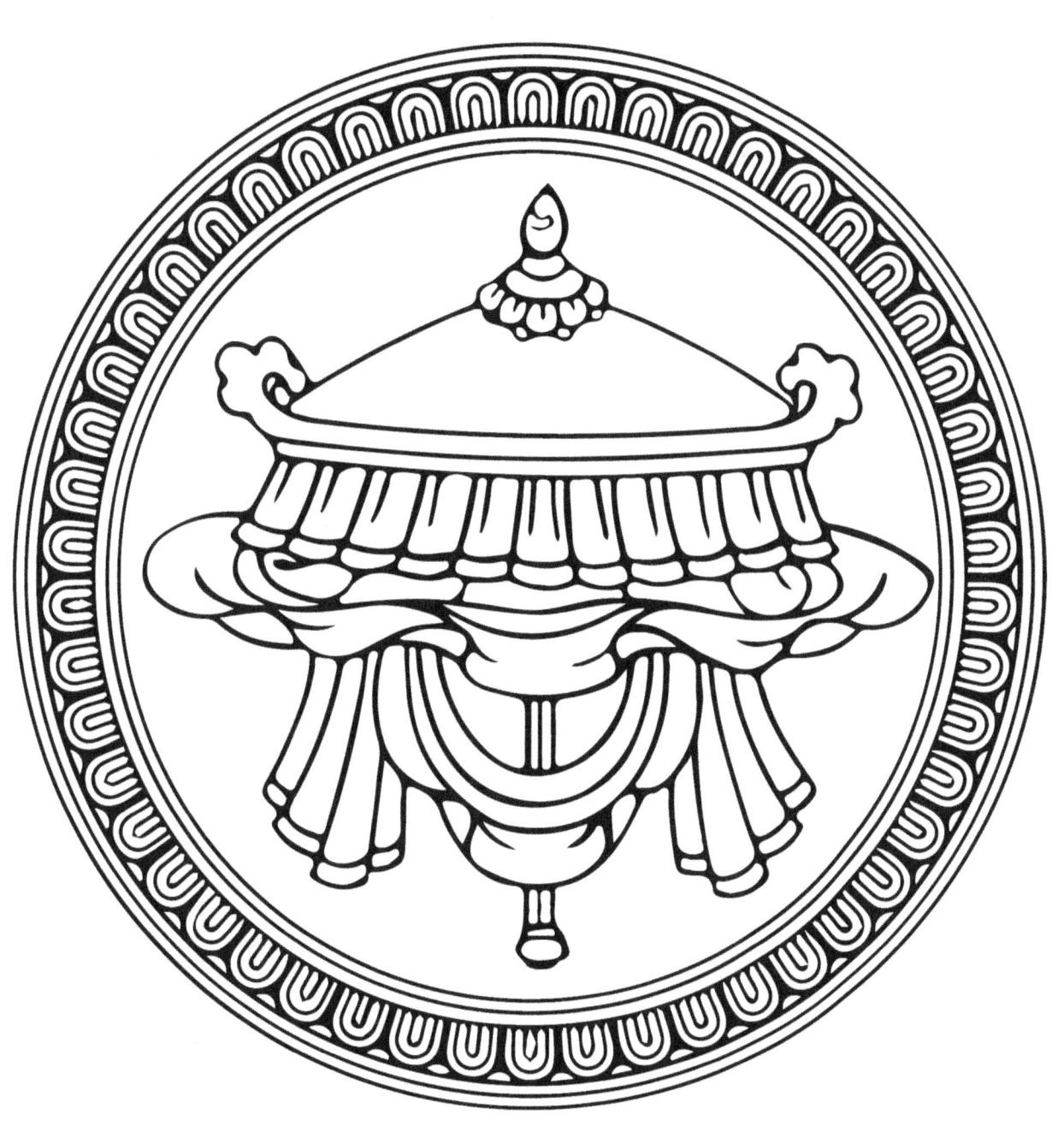

The Most Precious Parasol
Protects from suffering, destructive emotions, illness, harm and obstacles.

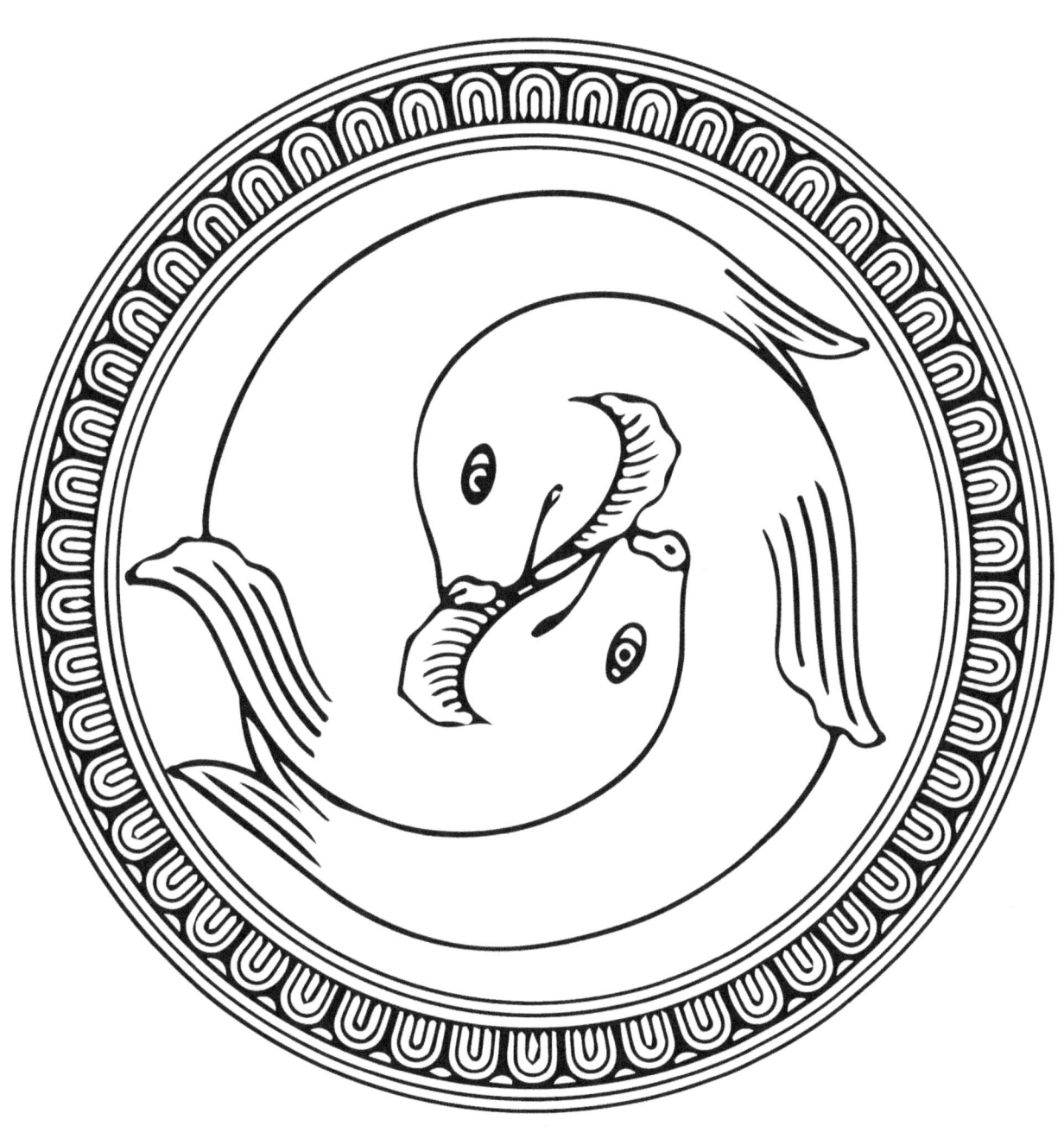

The Auspicious Golden Fishes

They stand for fearlessness, freedom and liberation, as well as happiness, fertility and abundance.

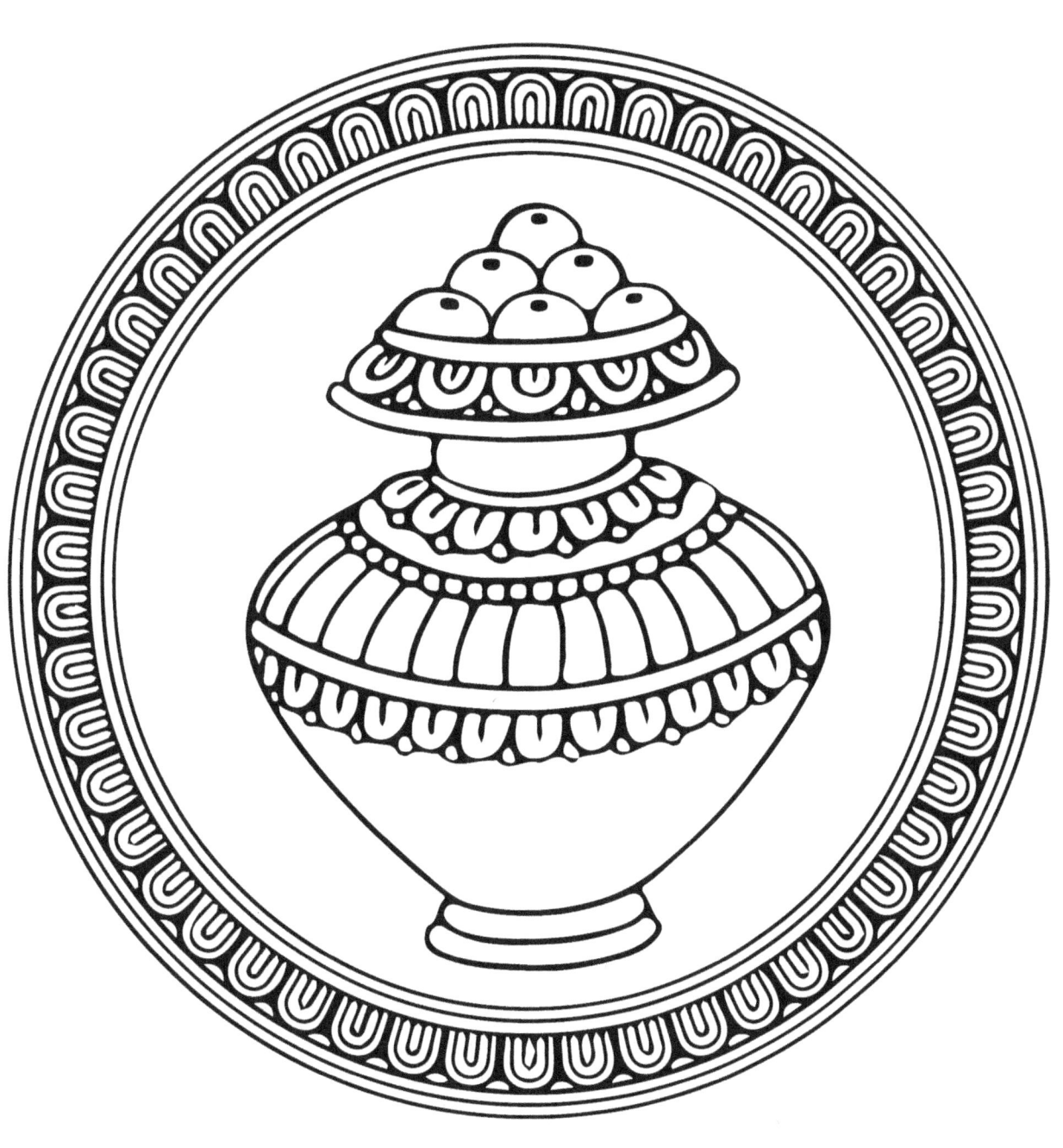

The Wish-fulfilling Vase of Treasure

An inexhaustible source of long life, wealth, and prosperity, which fulfils all one's spiritual and material wishes.

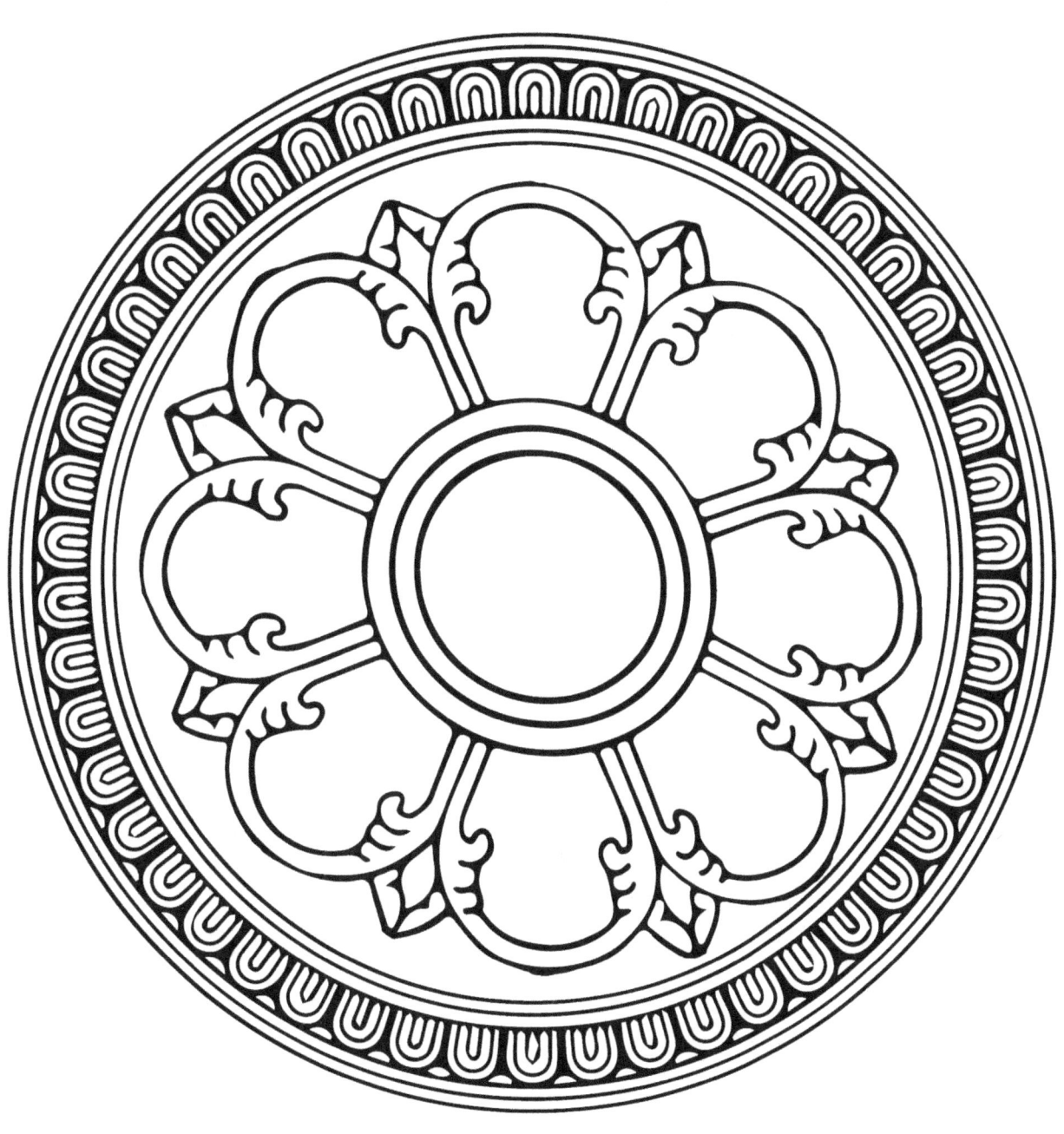

The Exquisite Lotus Blossom

Stands for purity of mind and heart, and transformation, as well as compassion, and all perfect qualities.

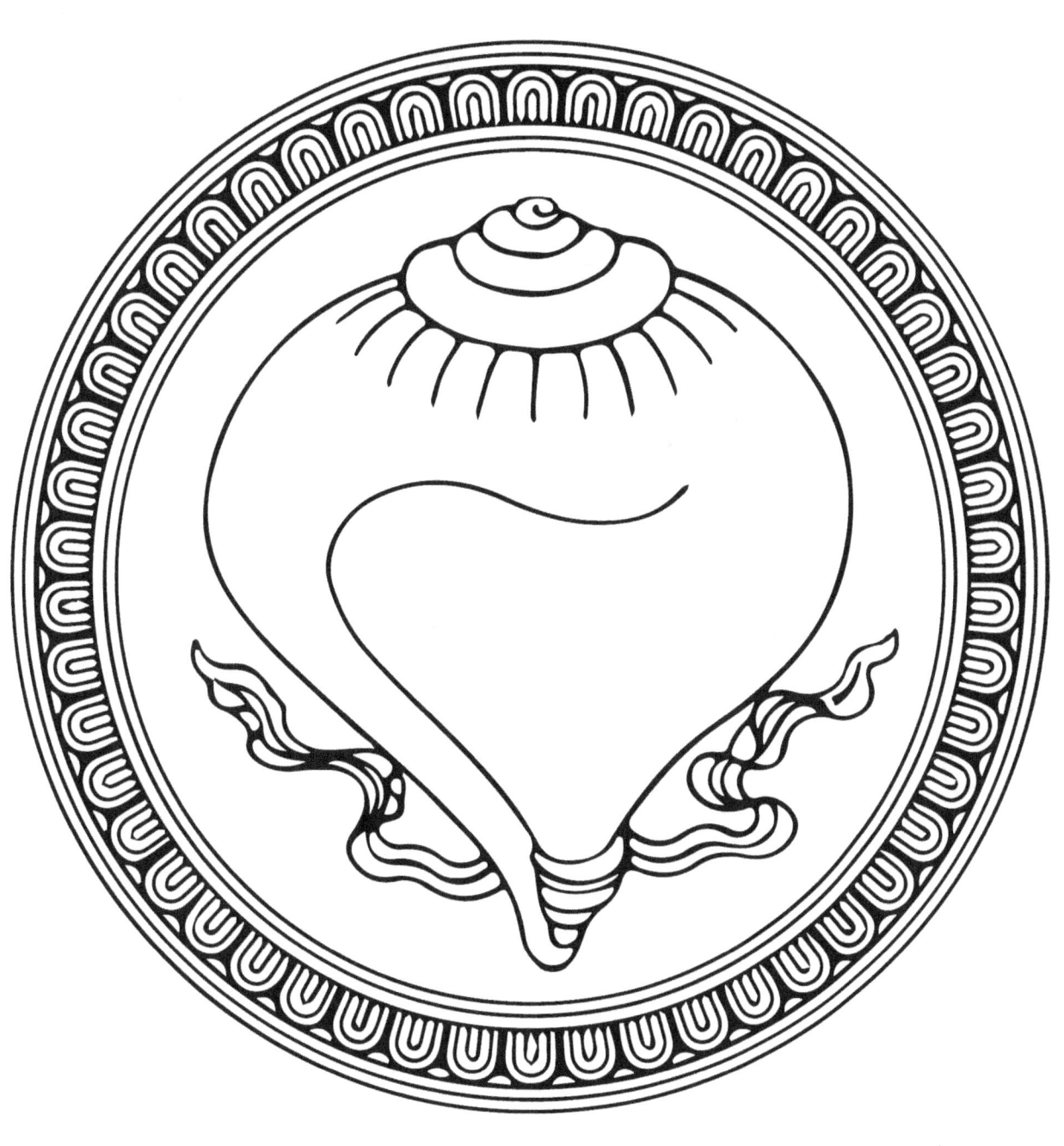

The Conch Shell of Far Renown

Symbolizes the far-reaching melodious sound of the spiritual teachings.

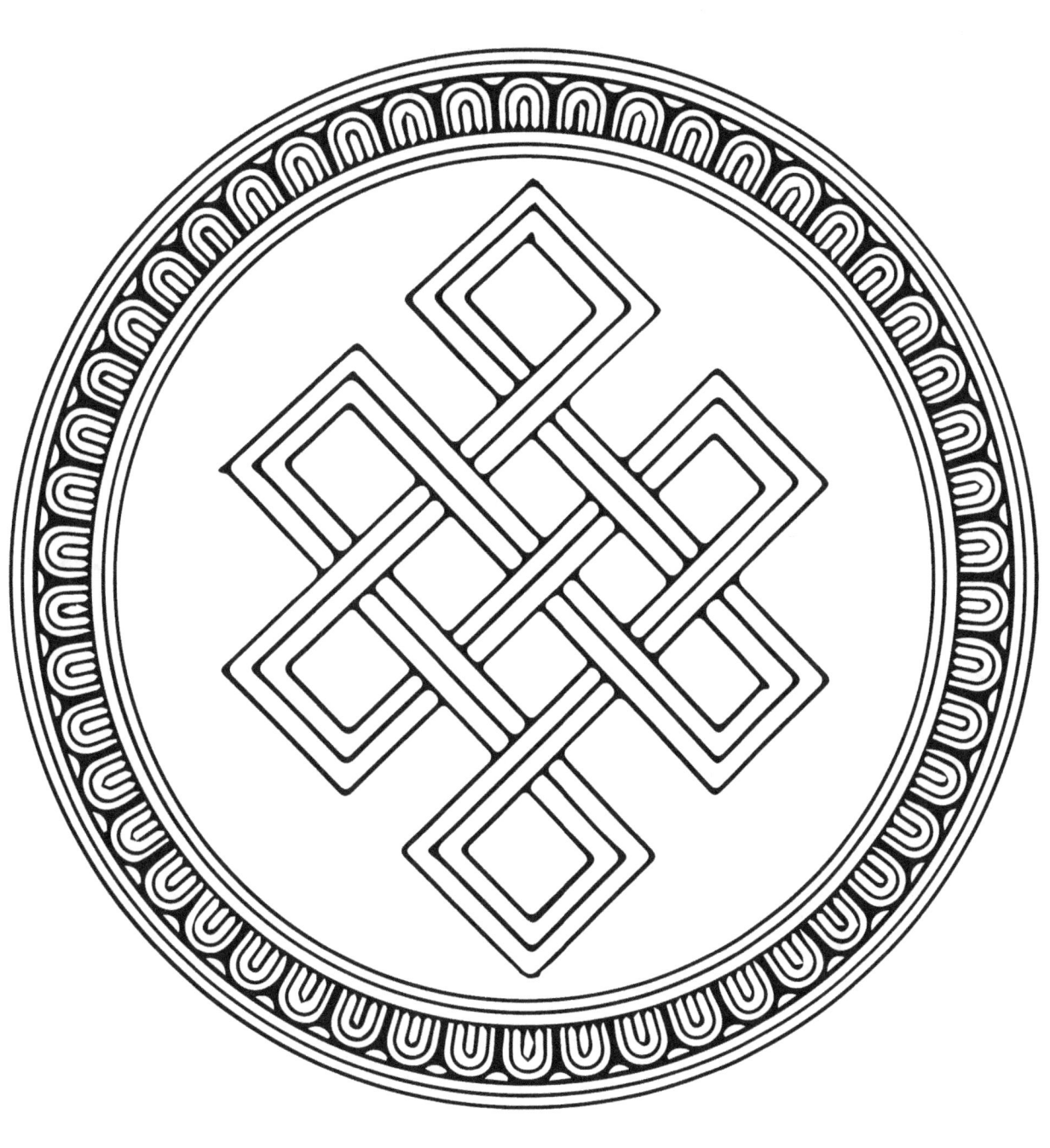

The Glorious Endless Knot

The sign of interdependence, of how everything in the universe is interconnected.

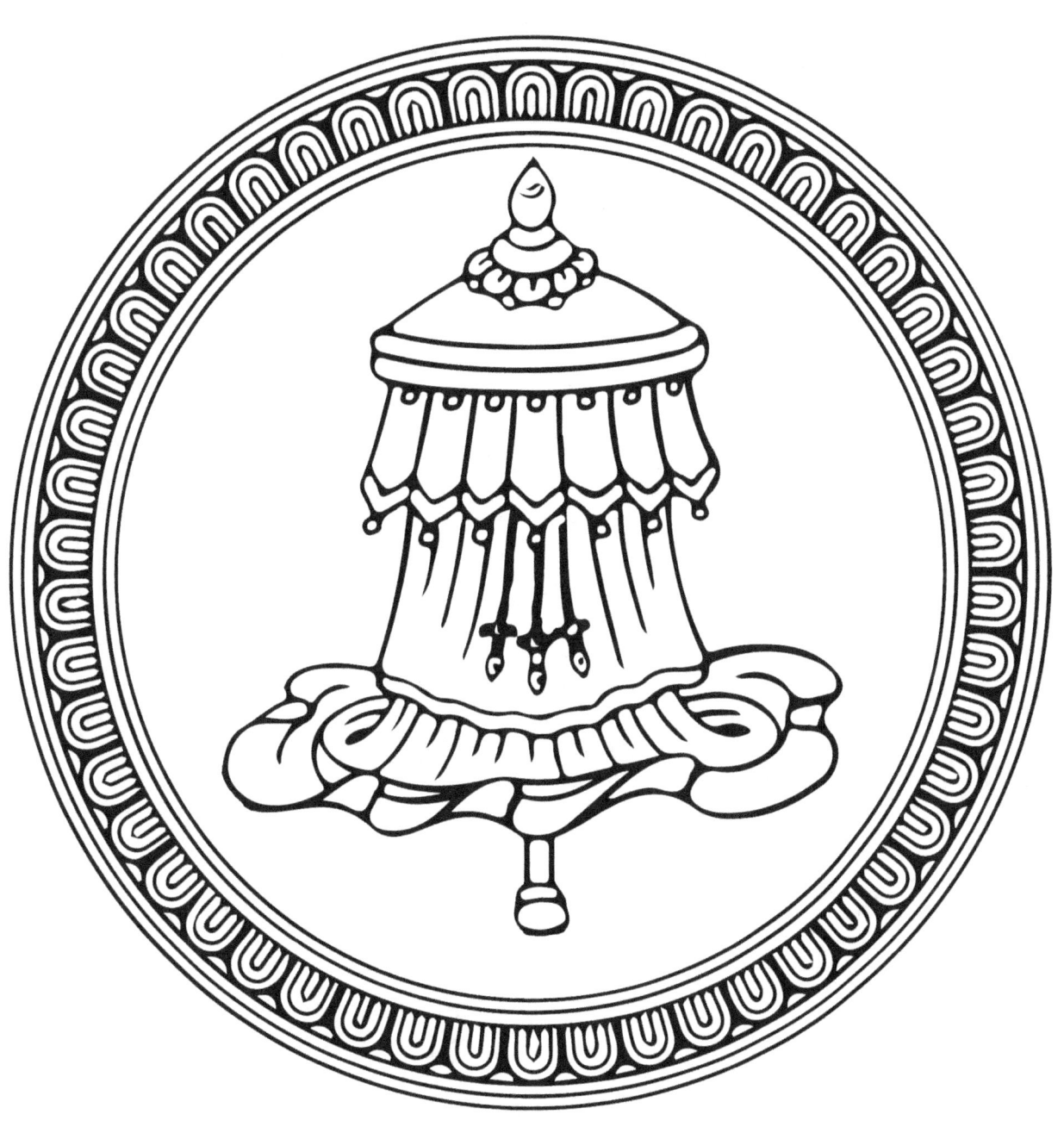

The Ever-Flying Banner of Victory

Means victory over all disagreement, disharmony or obstacles, and the attainment of happiness, both temporary and ultimate.

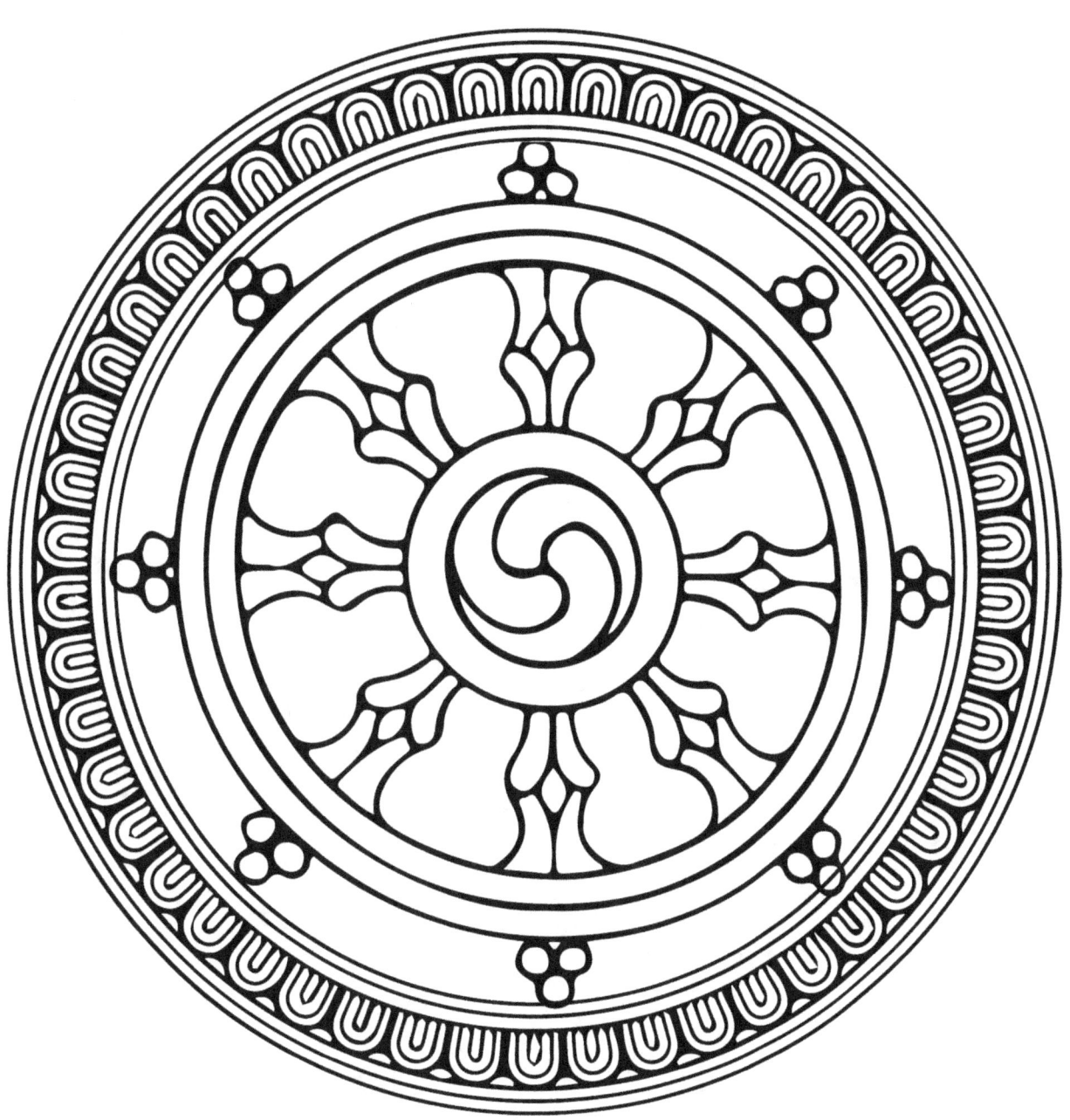

The All-powerful Wheel

Symbolizes the teaching of Buddha, and is the source of spiritual values, wealth, love and liberation.

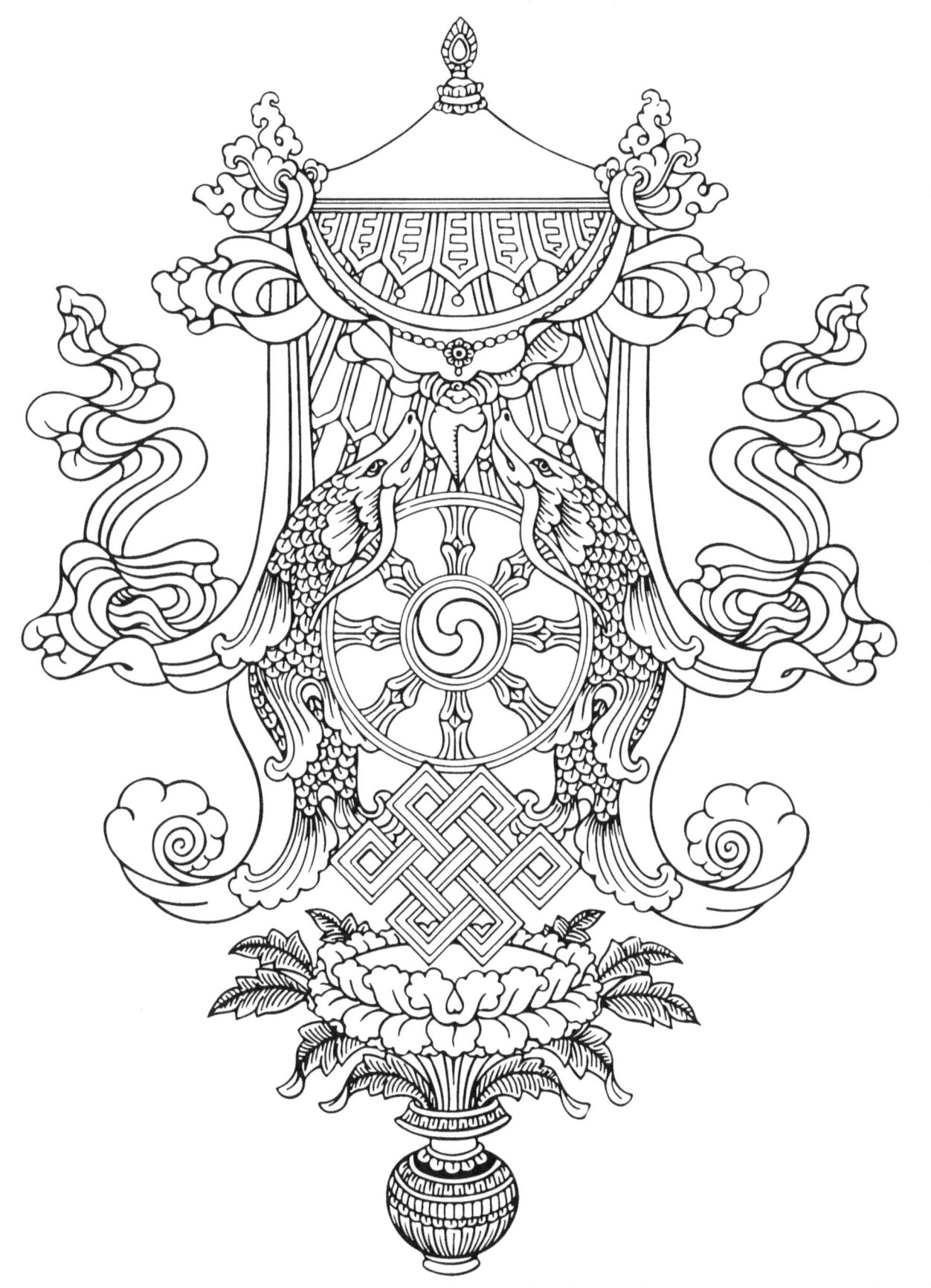

The Most Precious Parasol
Protects from suffering, destructive emotions, illness, harm and obstacles.

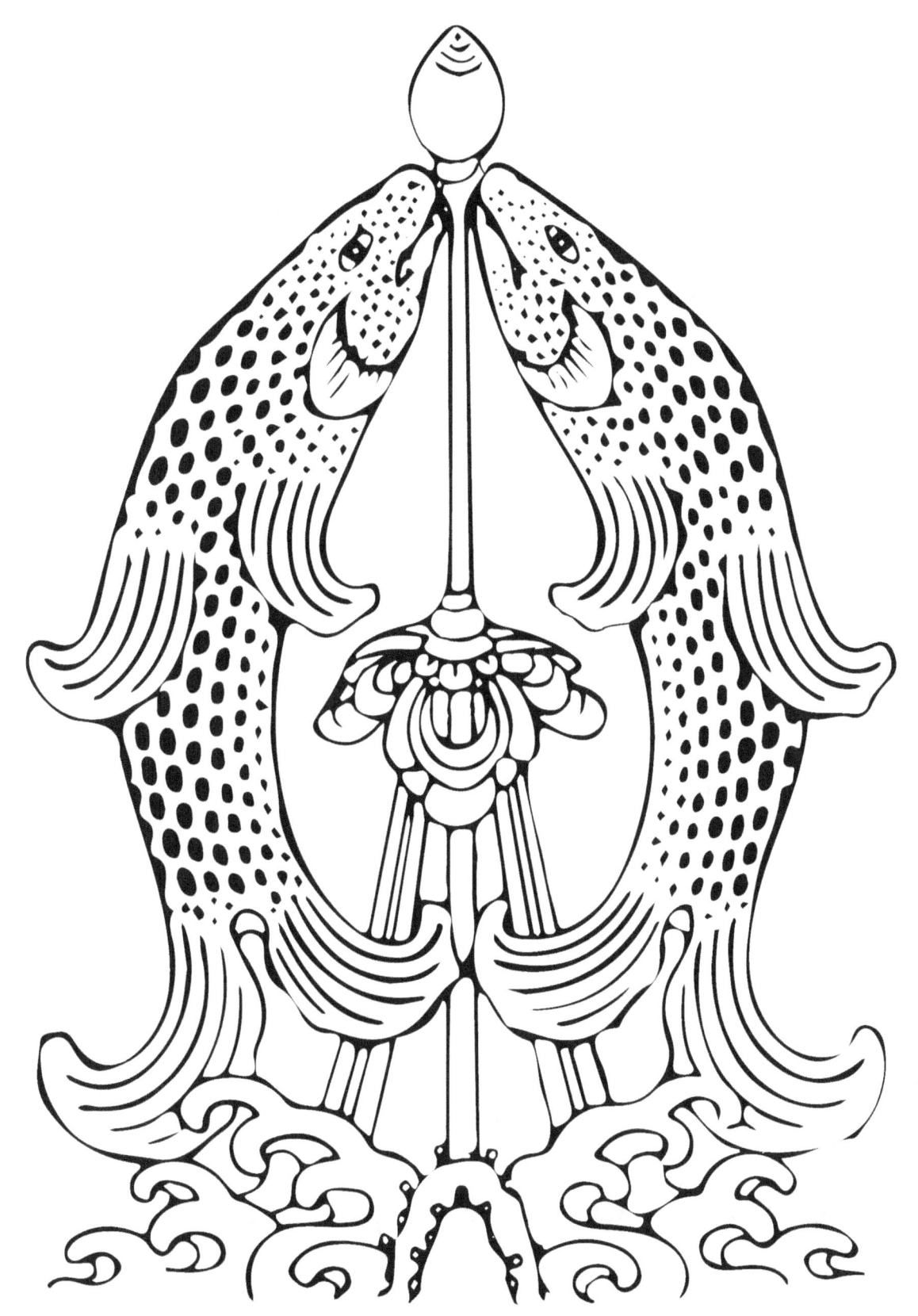

The Auspicious Golden Fishes

They stand for fearlessness, freedom and liberation, as well as happiness, fertility and abundance.

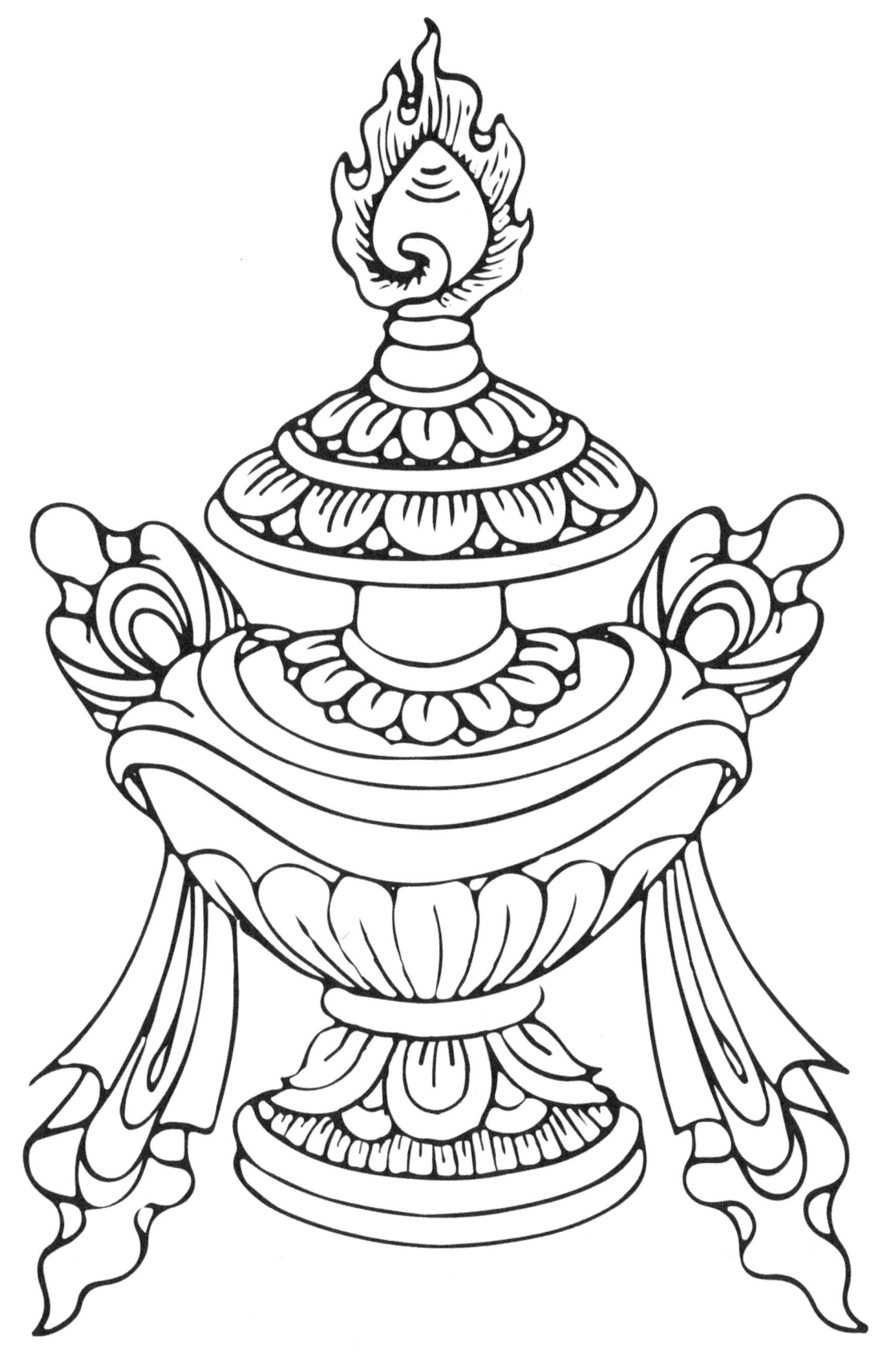

The Wish-fulfilling Vase of Treasure

An inexhaustible source of long life, wealth, and prosperity, which fulfils all one's spiritual and material wishes.

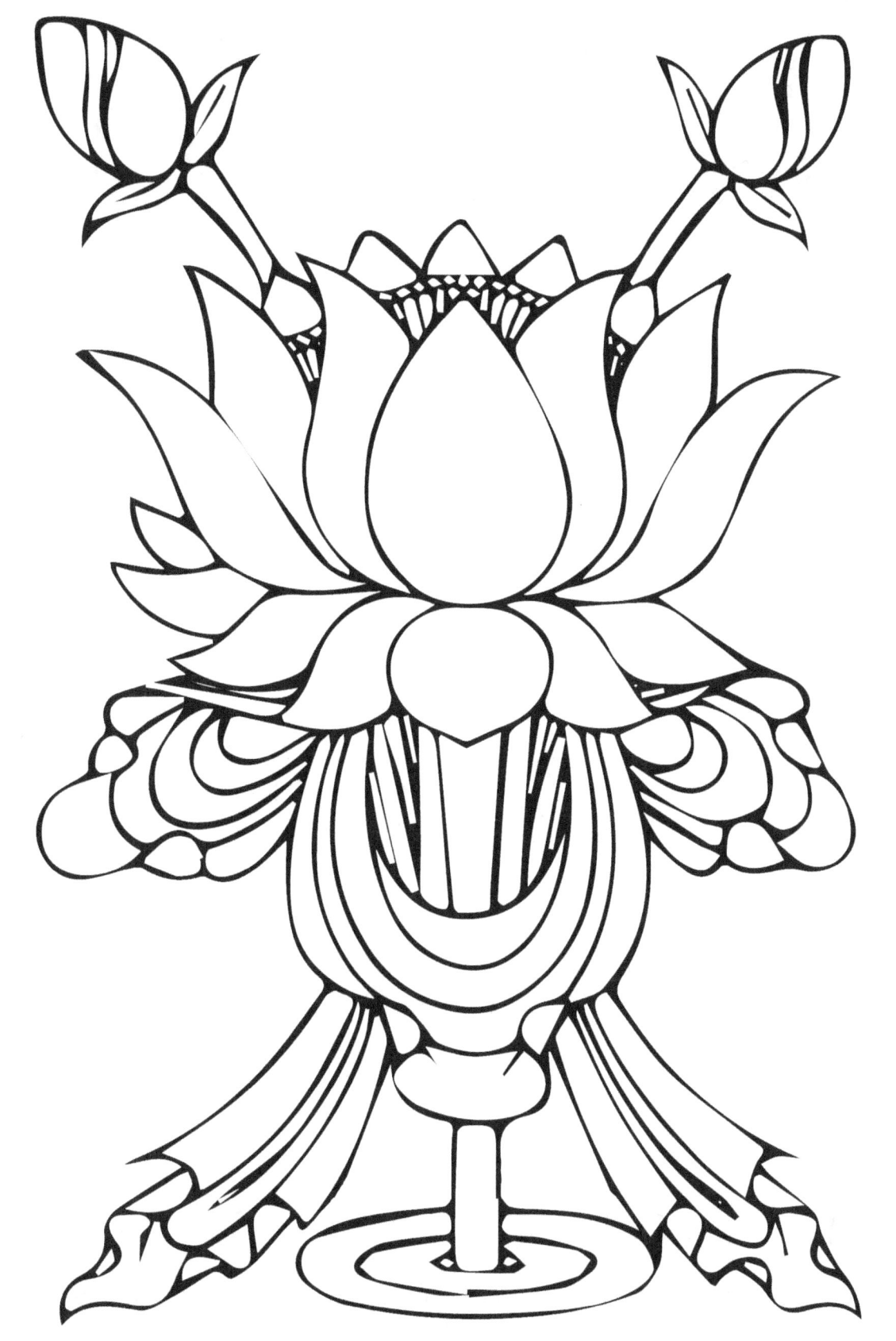

The Exquisite Lotus Blossom

Stands for purity of mind and heart, and transformation, as well as compassion, and all perfect qualities.

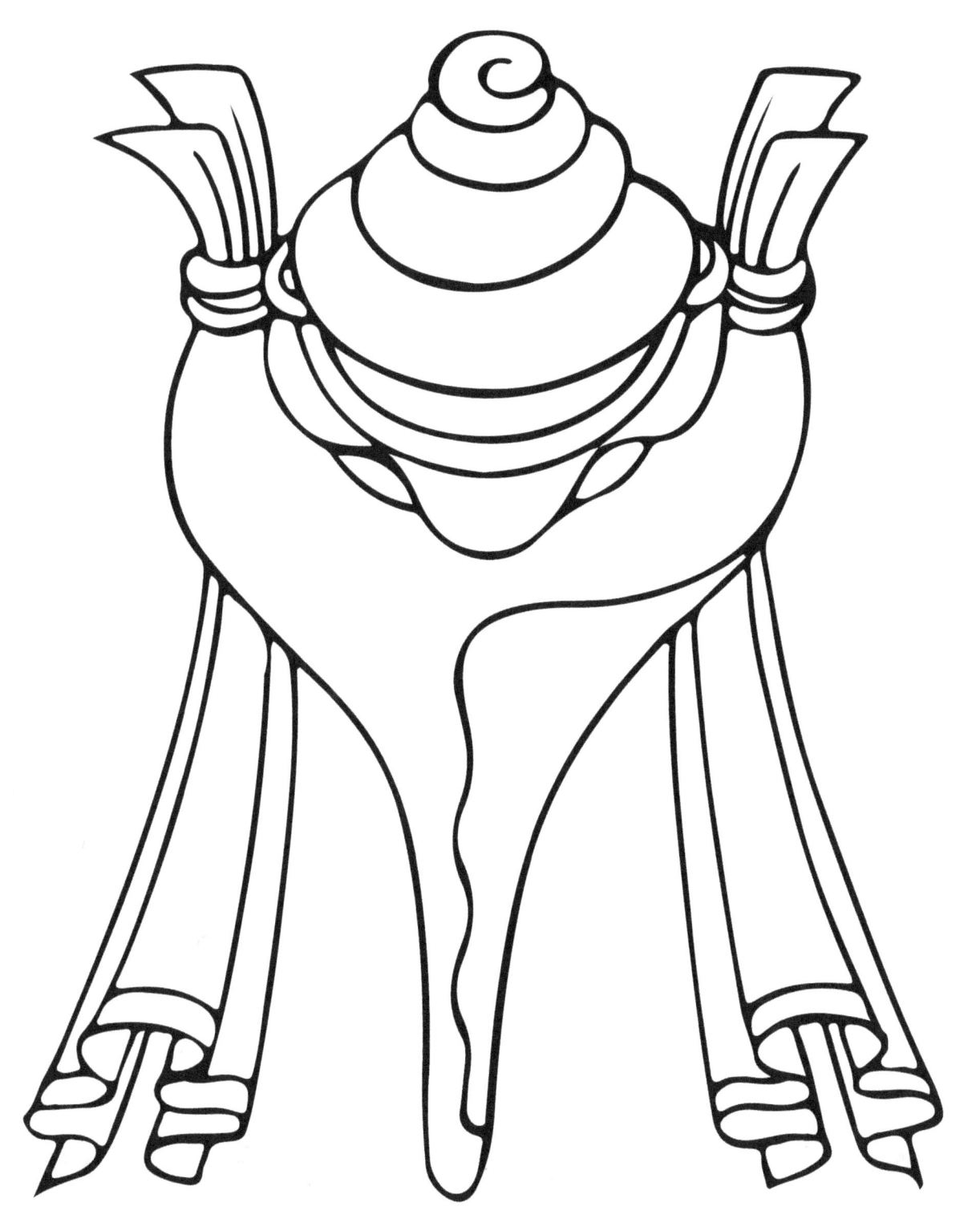

The Conch Shell of Far Renown

Symbolizes the far-reaching melodious sound of the spiritual teachings.

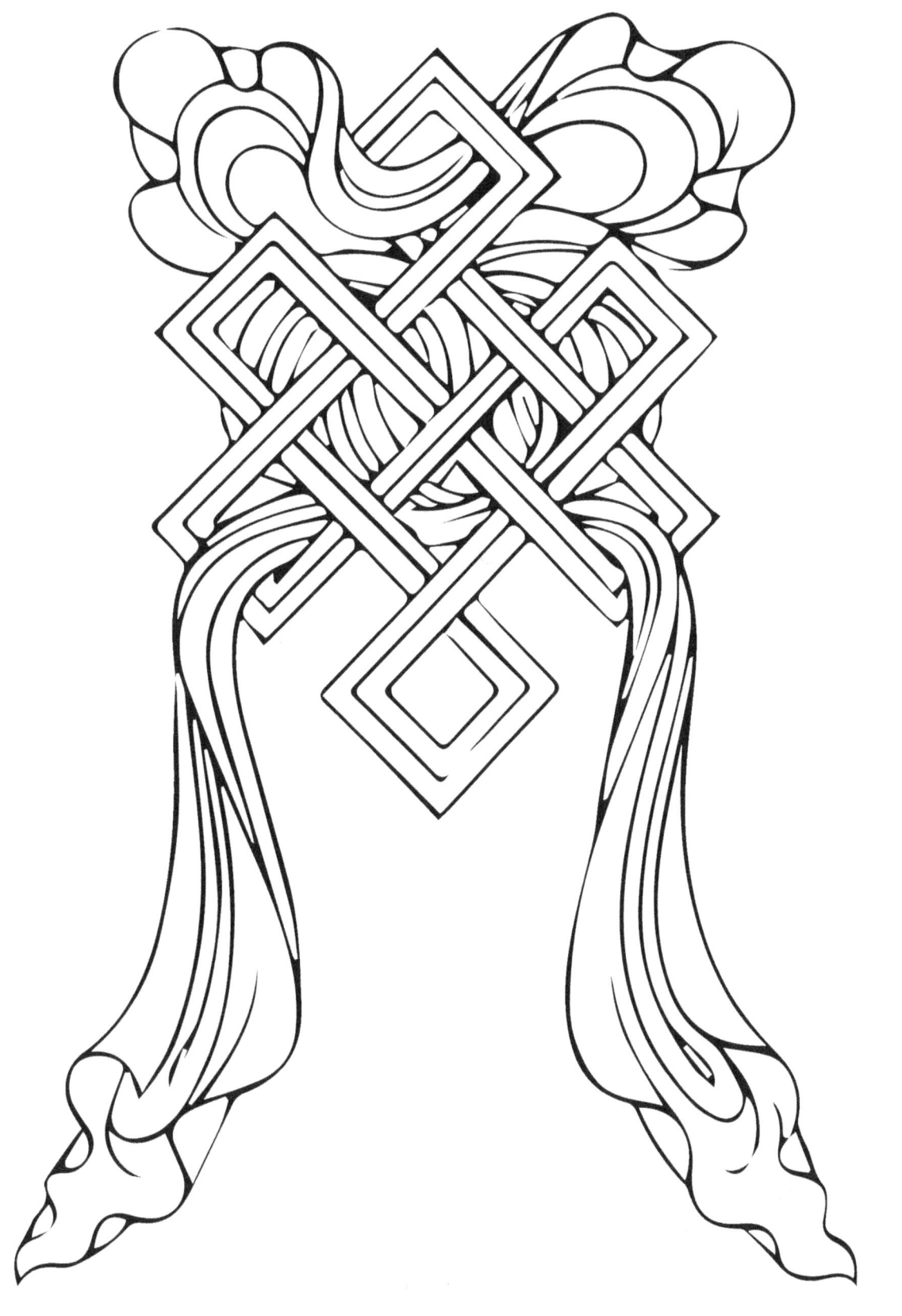

The Glorious Endless Knot

The sign of interdependence, of how everything in the universe is interconnected.

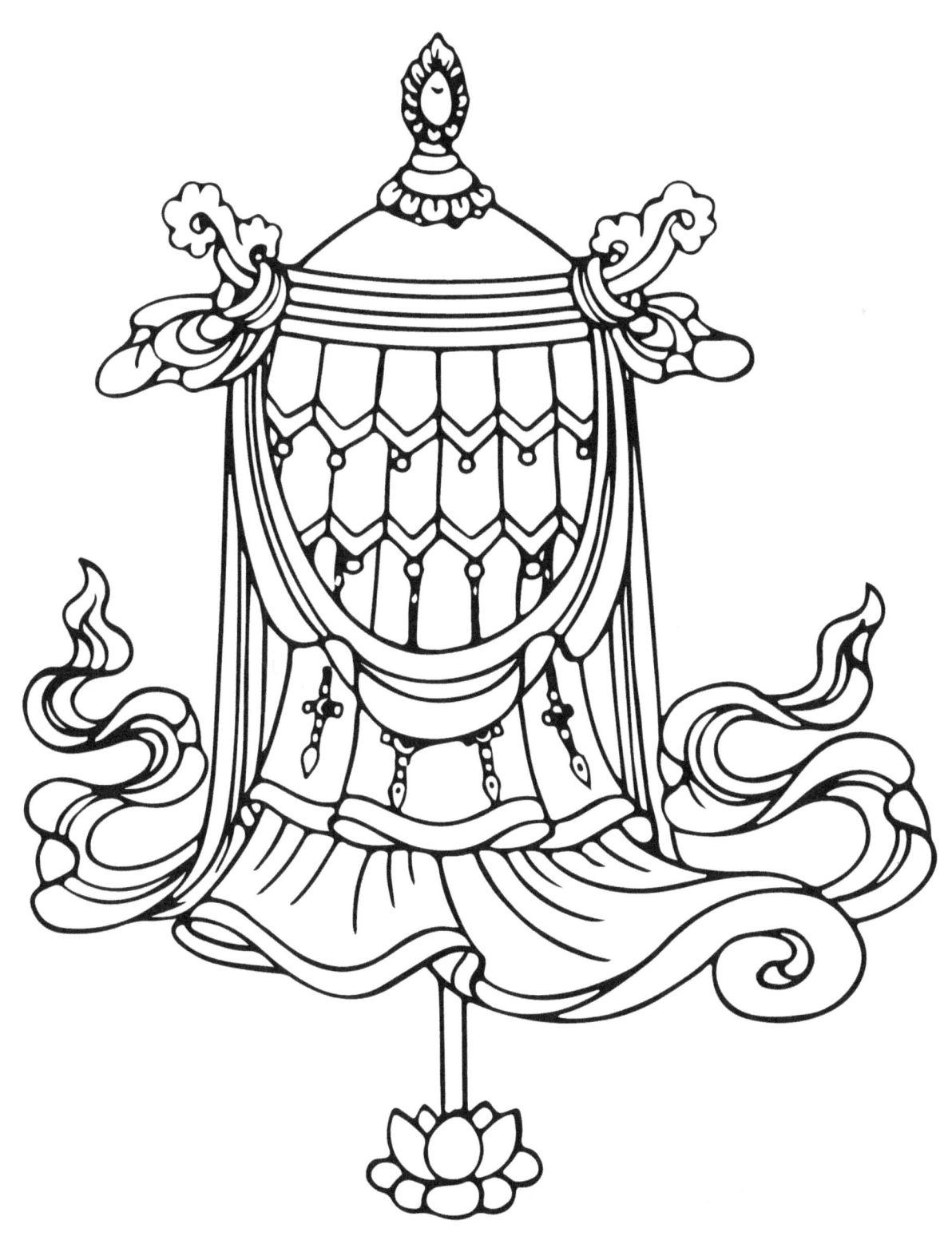

The Ever-Flying Banner of Victory

Means victory over all disagreement, disharmony or obstacles, and the attainment of happiness, both temporary and ultimate.

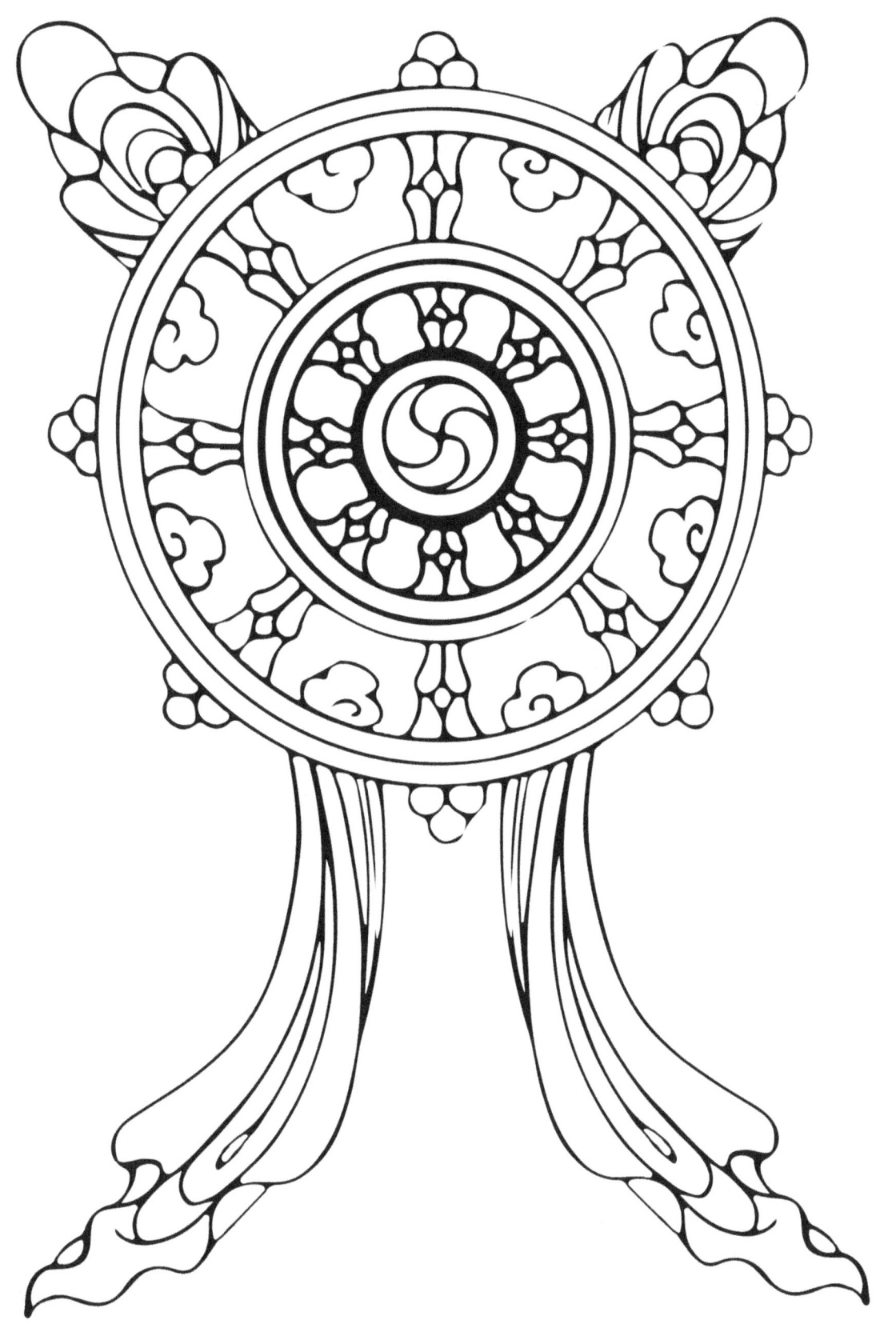

The All-powerful Wheel

Symbolizes the teaching of Buddha, and is the source of spiritual values, wealth, love and liberation.

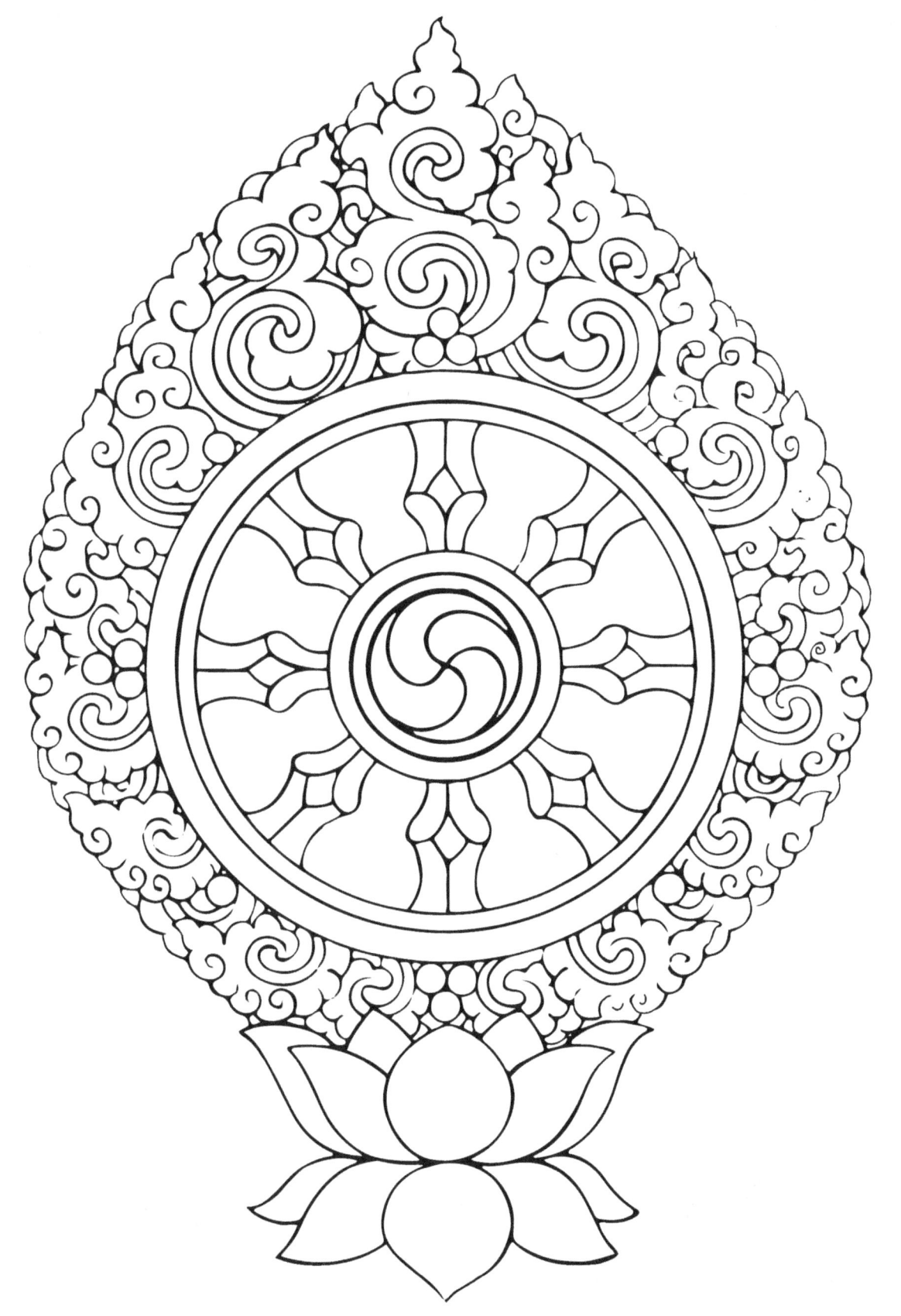

The All-powerful Wheel

Symbolizes the teaching of Buddha, and is the source of spiritual values, wealth, love and liberation.

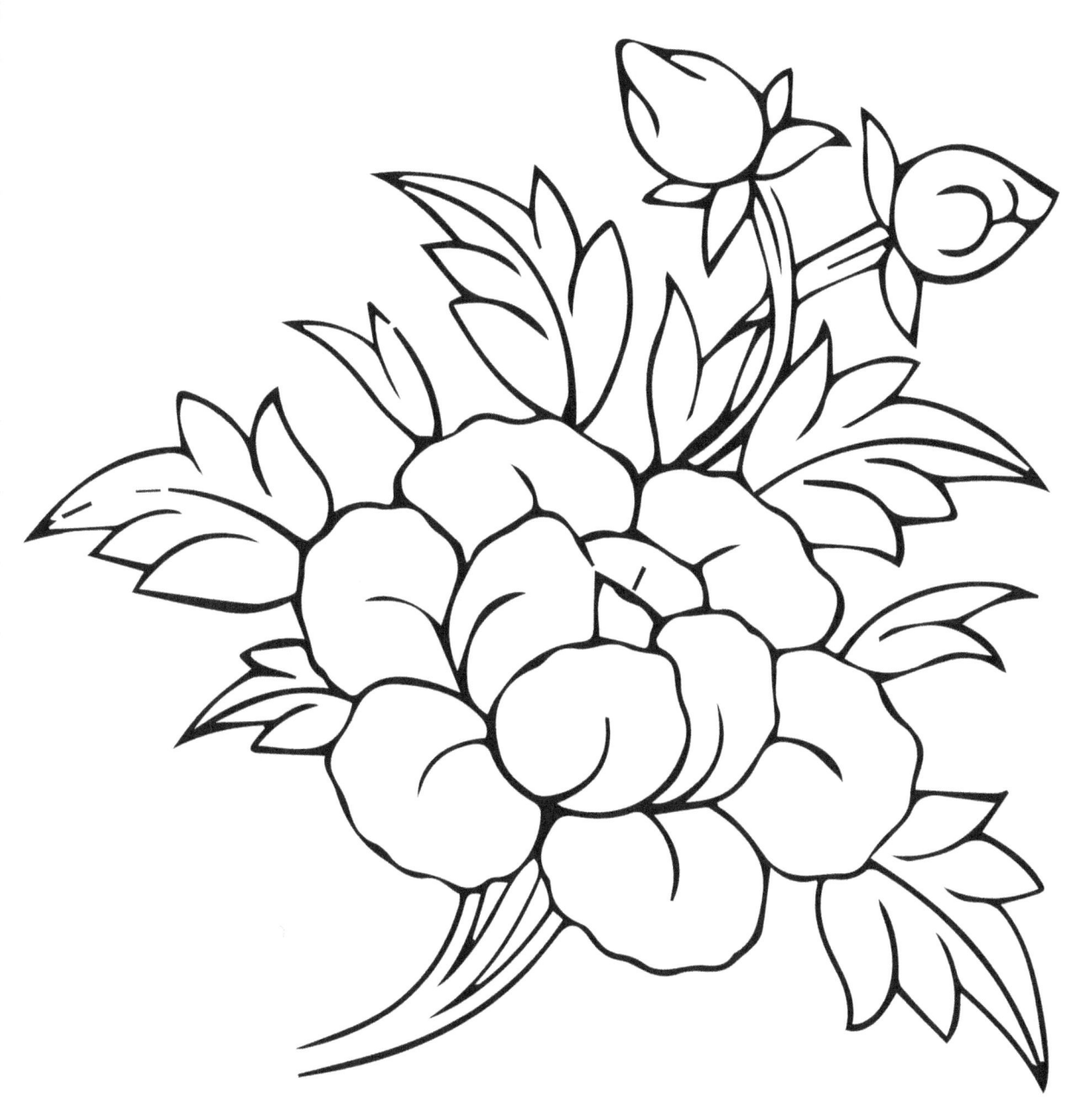

The Exquisite Lotus Blossom

Stands for purity of mind and heart, and transformation, as well as compassion, and all perfect qualities.

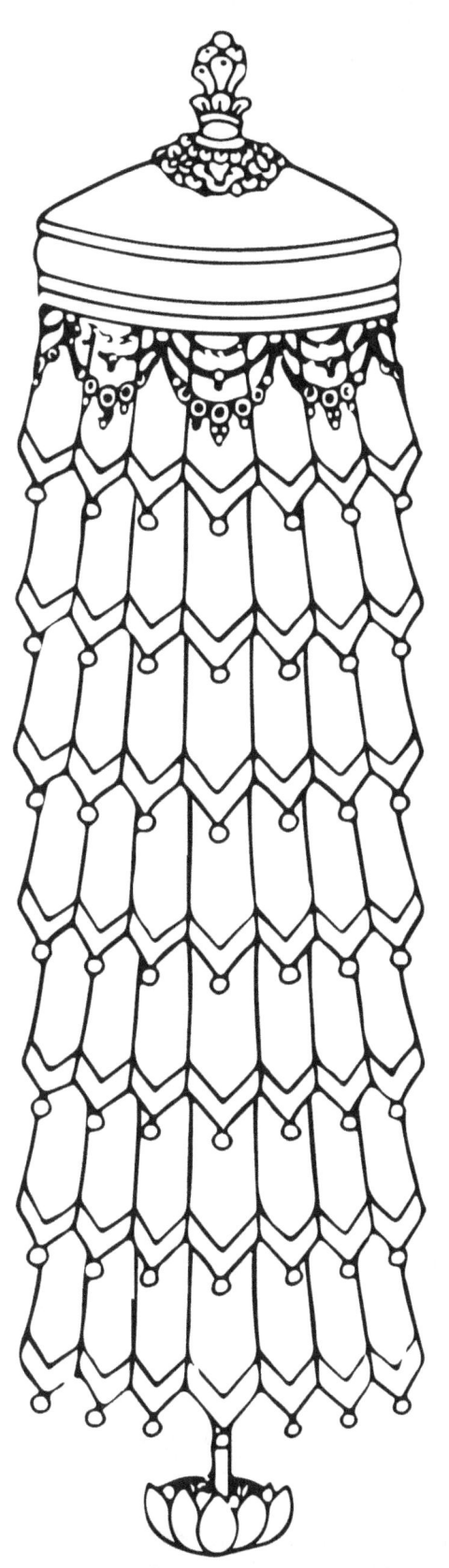

The Ever-Flying Banner of Victory

Means victory over all disagreement, disharmony or obstacles, and the attainment of happiness, both temporary and ultimate.

If you like this book, please leave a review and
check out other Pema Play books available on Amazon.com

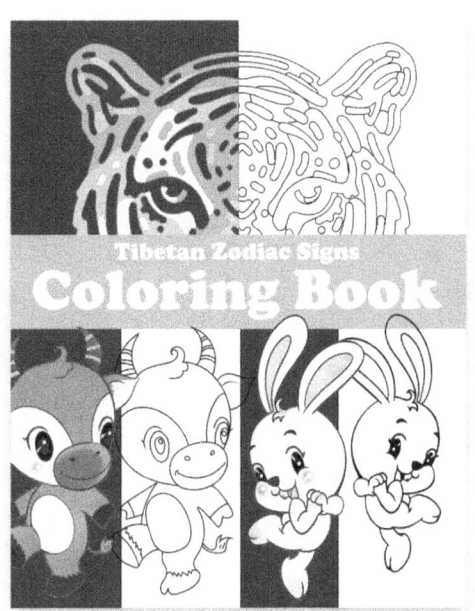

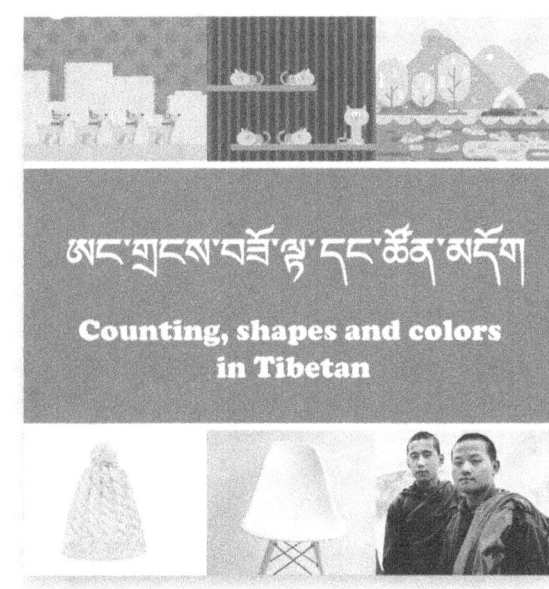

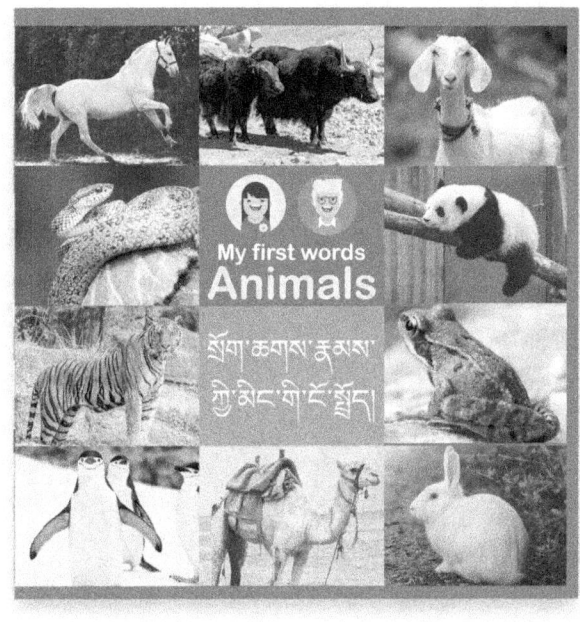

www.ingramcontent.com/pod-product-compliance
Lightning Source LLC
Chambersburg PA
CBHW081059240526
45465CB00025B/2771